cancer

OTHER BOOKS BY THE SAME AUTHORS

Illustrated by Andrew Antal

cancer

Alvin and Virginia Silverstein

The John Day Company · New York

Library of Congress Cataloging in Publication Data

Silverstein, Alvin.
    Cancer.

    SUMMARY: Explains the various forms of cancer, their symptoms, possible causes, and treatment, and discusses research being conducted to find better means of preventing, detecting, treating, and curing this disease.
    1. Cancer—Juvenile literature. [1. Cancer]
I. Silverstein, Virginia B., joint author.
II. Antal, Andrew, illus.   III. Title.
RC263.S49   616.9′94   74-155010

ISBN: 0-381-99708-1 RB

Designed by The Etheredges
Manufactured in the United States of America

10 9 8 7 6 5 4

*To the memory of
Representative John Fogarty,
who did much to
foster medical research.*

contents

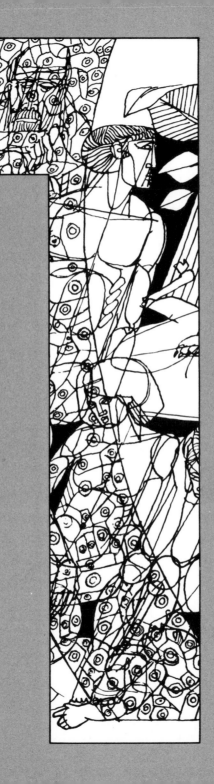

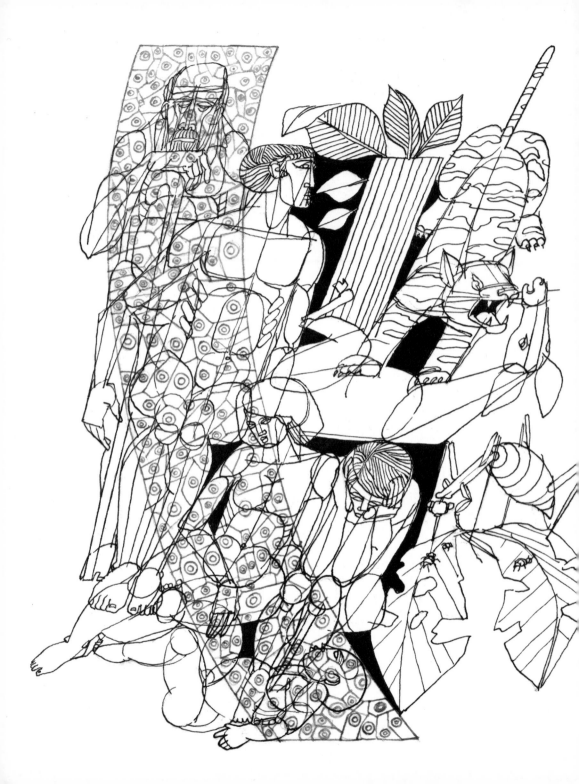

a world of life and death

All creatures born upon this earth must, in the end, die. Some live long and peaceful lives. But others are caught up in struggles—must fight for their lives.

In a quiet meadow, down amid the swaying grasses, a praying mantis is pouncing upon a family of *aphids* (AY-fidz). These plump little insects in turn are sucking away at the juices of the plant on which they are perched. And the leaves of the plant are already wilted. Nearby a grazing deer is nibbling away at the grass. Suddenly there is a flash as the tawny body of a bobcat leaps through the air and brings the unsuspecting deer crashing to the ground.

Scenes of struggles for life and death are repeated over and over each day, in the jungles, in the deserts, in the seas—everywhere there is life. Enemies lurk all about, and even within. When tiny *bacteria* (back-TEER-ee-uh) or even smaller *viruses* (VYE-russ-ez) attack an animal or plant, that creature may become sick, or diseased. Every living creature has its own set of diseases, its own enemies that can cause it harm or even end its life.

Many millions of people die each year from *malaria* (ma-LAIR-ee-uh). This disease is caused by a tiny animal-like creature that is actually injected into the blood by mosquitoes when they bite people. Bacteria and viruses cause many millions of people to die each year throughout the world from hundreds of different kinds of diseases, such as pneumonia and influenza, diphtheria, typhoid fever, cholera, and smallpox. In this country, the biggest cause of death is the diseases that affect the heart and blood vessels. In these ailments the person's own body fails him, and some important part such as the heart no longer works properly. These are called *degenerative* (dee-JEN-er-eh-tiv) diseases, and they strike mainly older people.

The second biggest killer in this country is cancer. It is thought by many to be the most terrible disease in the world. It strikes people of all ages—newborn babies, boys and girls, and men and women.

Just what is cancer? We don't really know. We have learned a lot *about* cancer, and we know some of the things that can cause cancer. We are learning ways to avoid getting cancer, and scientists are following many promising pathways in search of a cure for this disease.

But before we can talk about what cancer is and discuss the exciting discoveries that are being made in cancer research laboratories throughout the world, we must find out more about how the normal body works.

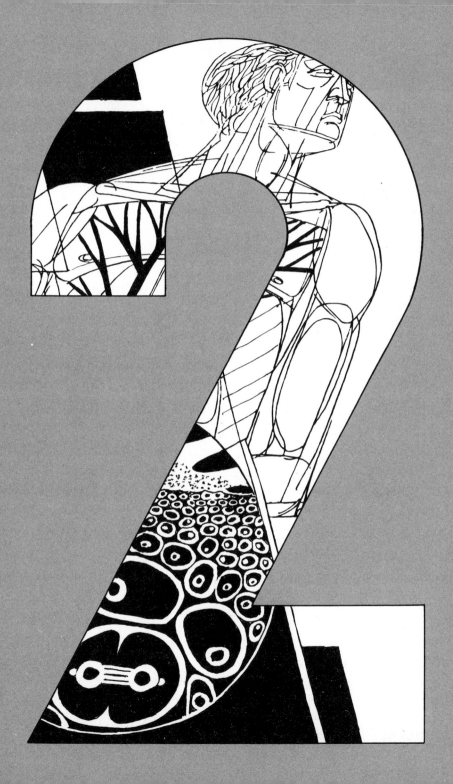

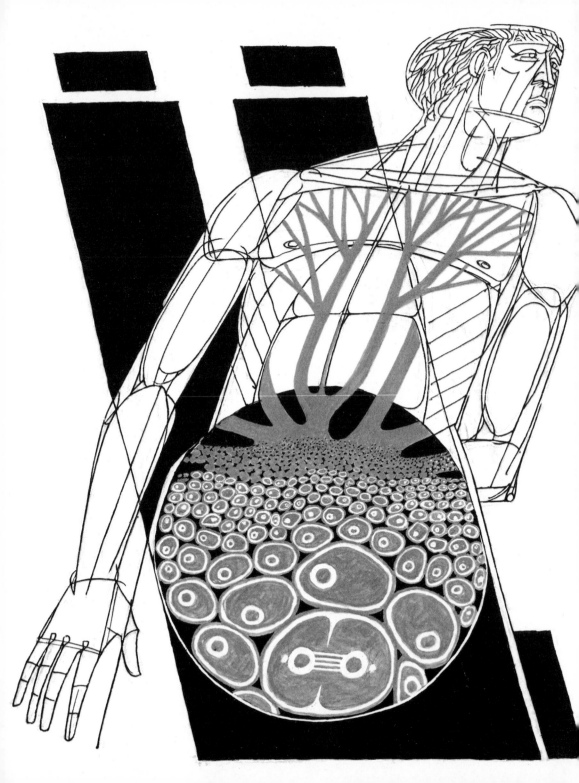

from cell to man

A human being is a most wondrous thing. He can dream and plan, smile and laugh, walk and run. His body has grown from an invisible speck to a smoothly running "machine" far more complicated than any man has made.

The parts of the body work in a beautiful harmony. Each depends upon the others. The heart pumps the blood that feeds the lungs and the kidneys, the hands and the feet. The lungs in turn bring in fresh oxygen that helps to burn the fuel that the stomach and intestines have digested. The kidneys remove the poisons that are formed from the burned fuel.

The heart, the lungs, the kidneys—indeed, the whole body

—is made up of far smaller building blocks, the cells. Cells come in a great variety of sizes and shapes. Those in the lining of the cheeks look like miniature pavement stones. The nerve cells that link the various parts of the body in a communications network look like long threads. The trillions of red blood cells that float through the bloodstream look like tiny doughnuts without the hole in the middle.

Each cell is a busy factory. Thousands of different chemicals react with each other to form new substances, which help the cells live and do their own special jobs. Nerve cells carry messages that permit us to see and hear and think. Muscle cells work with nerve cells to help us move. Red blood cells carry oxygen to all the other cells of the body. White blood cells help to fight disease germs.

Each cell is surrounded by a very thin covering, like a plastic bag. This is the *cell membrane* (MEM-brain). It is a rather unusual covering. It lets only certain chemicals through and keeps out others. Some scientists think the cell membrane plays a very important role in cancer.

The inside of the cell is divided into many smaller compartments by a network of membranes that seem to branch off from the cell membrane. Within these compartments is a fluid called the *cytoplasm* (SYE-toe-plazm), within which chemicals and other tiny structures are found.

The *nucleus* (NUE-klee-us) is a structure within the cell that controls many of its activities. Within the nucleus is a substance called *DNA* (DEE-EN-AY), which makes up the most important parts of the *genes* (JEENZ). It is the genes that contain the complete plans for the body. Genes determine whether you will have blue eyes or brown, whether you will have two legs or four, hair or feathers or scales. Genes send out information that tells the cell what chemicals to make, how much, and when to make them. Indeed, most scientists feel that cancer comes about when something goes wrong with the DNA, and the messages the genes give out are the wrong kind for the normal life of the cell. And when the cell divides into two, each new daughter cell also carries the same abnormal DNA, which sends out the same set of wrong messages. All the generations of cells that follow will also carry this changed DNA. If the new messages include instructions that tell the cell to divide more rapidly or more often than normal cells, then a growing mass of cells or tissue will form. This is *cancer* (CAN-ser).

what is cancer?

Cancer is growth run wild. This growth occurs in two ways. The cells get larger, and when they reach a certain size they divide in two. Normal cells do this also. Indeed, growth and cell division are a necessary part of life—all life. Even when the body itself has stopped growing, many of its cells continue to grow and divide to replace those that have died or worn out. A red blood cell lives about four months, and a white blood cell lives only a week or so. Cells of our skin are constantly being worn off and replaced by new cells.

Normal cells stop growing after a while or grow only at a rather slow pace. Scientists have found that when the cell

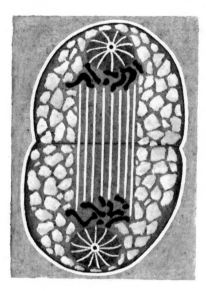

A normal cell dividing

membranes of two normal cells touch each other, they both stop growing. Somehow each gives the other a signal that turns off the DNA that controls cell growth and division. But when two cancer cells touch, somehow the signal is not given or is not received properly. The DNA is not turned off, and the cancer cells continue to grow and divide. They pile up in an untidy heap, one on top of the other. They can even invade nearby normal tissues. The normal cells are held together by a sort of glue. But cancer cells give off, or secrete, a certain chemical that seems to dissolve the glue. Then the cancer cells can squeeze in among the normal cells and spread through them. They form a growing lump of cancerous tissue called a *tumor* (TUE-mer).

Sometimes a tumor reaches a certain size and then stops growing. Somehow the cells seem to obey the normal contact signals again. A tumor that stops growing in this way is called a *benign* (bee-NINE) tumor.

But some tumors continue to grow and spread. These are called *malignant* (ma-LIG-nent) tumors. They may grow to the size of a grapefruit or even larger.

Often a clump of cancer cells will break away and be carried along in the bloodstream. Sometimes these cancer cells may take root in different parts of the body and begin to grow there too. This migration of cancer cells through the bloodstream is called *metastasis* (meh-TASS-ta-sis).

How did the cancer cells get started in the first place? What changed their DNA? Scientists are not sure exactly how this happens. They do know that certain chemicals cause cancer. They also know that many kinds of cancers in animals are caused by viruses and they suspect that this is true of some or even most of the cancers that are found in man. If indeed it is found that viruses do cause human cancers, then scientists will be able to make *vaccines* (vac-SEENZ) to protect people from cancer. Vaccines are already protecting people from virus diseases such as smallpox, influenza, and polio.

Some scientists believe that it is a combination of certain chemicals and viruses that changes a normal cell into a cancer cell. A virus is a very simple kind of living thing. Its inner part is made of DNA or sometimes another, similar chemical called *RNA* (AR-EN-AY). A *protein* (PRO-teen) coat surrounds the inner part. When a virus invades a cell, just the DNA enters the cell, leaving the protein coat outside. The DNA of a virus looks very much like the normal DNA in the cell. Until recently scientists could not tell the difference between them. But now they have devised a method to tell whether or not part of the DNA within a human cell came from a virus. They are using this technique to try to find out whether viruses cause cancers in human beings.

Robert Huebner, a leading cancer researcher who is working at the National Cancer Institute, believes that a virus may remain in human cells for many years without doing anything. Suddenly some chemical or *radiation* (ray-dee-AY-shun) such as X-rays or even the *ultraviolet* (ul-truh-VYE-oh-let) rays from sunlight might "awaken" this virus into action so that it causes cancer.

Other scientists do not think that viruses are involved in human cancers. Instead, they believe that the chemicals themselves change the DNA of the normal cell so that it becomes a cancer cell. Indeed, many of these chemicals, which are called *carcinogens* (car-SIN-oh-jenz), have been shown to change DNA in test tubes.

There are still many unanswered questions about how cancer is caused; these questions must be answered if cancer is to be conquered.

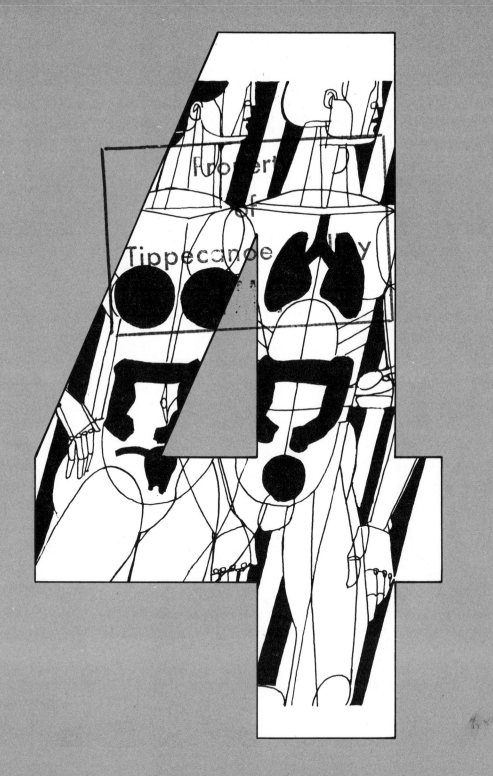

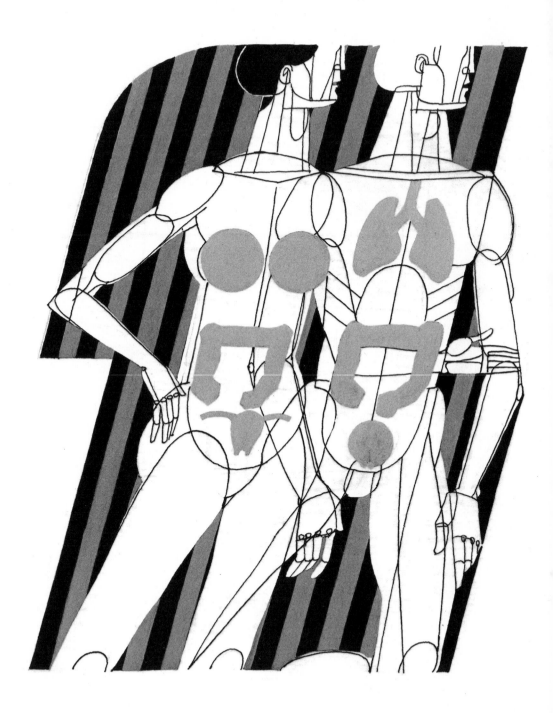

kinds of cancer

Cancer is still a great mystery, even though it strikes almost all the different kinds of animals in the world. In fact, plants too can come down with cancer.

Cancer is not just one disease. In man alone, scientists think that there are dozens or even more than a hundred different kinds of cancer. This disease may strike almost any part of the body: skin, lungs, intestines, breast, brain, mouth, bones, and blood.

Scientists use many different kinds of names when they talk about cancers. The names you will see most in the newspapers are carcinoma, sarcoma, and leukemia.

A *carcinoma* (car-sin-OH-muh) is a cancer that starts in covering tissues. It occurs in the skin and the inner and outer coverings of the breathing passages and lungs and of the digestive system from the mouth down through the stomach and intestines. Cancers of the brain, nerves, liver, and glands and some kinds of bone cancers are also carcinomas.

Sarcomas (sar-KOH-muhz) are cancers that begin in connective tissue found beneath the skin and between and within organs and glands of the body. Sarcomas are found in *cartilage* (CAR-ti-ledj), a tough gristle that gives shape to your ears and helps to support the bones of your spine. Tumors of muscle and fatty tissue are called sarcomas. This type also includes some bone and nerve cancers.

Leukemias (lue-KEE-mee-uhz) are the blood cancers. In these cancers the body makes too many white blood cells. In the normal body there is only about one white blood cell for every 600 red blood cells. When a person has leukemia, his blood may have as many as 10, 20, or even 100 white blood cells for every 600 red blood cells.

The white blood cells are made by yellow bone marrow cells inside hollows in some of the bones. In leukemia these yellow bone marrow cells become malignant. They divide again and again, producing far too many white blood cells. Most of these white blood cells never develop completely or mature. The yellow bone marrow cells spread and crowd out the nearby red bone marrow, which makes red blood cells. That is why leukemia patients suffer from *anemia* (a-NEE-mee-uh)—they do not have enough red blood cells. And because the chemistry of the blood is upset, the patients bleed easily. For these reasons they must receive many blood transfusions.

Thousands of people each year get leukemia and many of these are children. Although a number of drugs and other treatments have been developed, there is not yet a real cure for this disease. Some of the most effective drugs cause nearly all of the leukemia cells to disappear from the blood. This kind of temporary recovery is called a *remission* (ree-MISH-un). It may last for months or even years. But then the cancerous bone marrow cells begin to multiply wildly again. And soon the patient dies.

Most cancers are what is known as "solid tumors." In other words, the cancer is a solid mass of tissues. These tumors can appear in almost any part of the body. In women, they occur most often in the breast as a solid lump, and in the *uterus* (YEW-ter-us), the organ where a baby develops before it is born. Doctors advise women to check their breasts for lumps every now and then. If they find a lump, they should see the doctor right away. There is a very simple and good test for cancers of the uterus. This is called the *Pap smear*, from the name of Dr. George Papanicolaou, who developed it. The doctor wipes the entrance to the uterus with a small cotton swab. Thousands of cells that have already broken away from the tissues are picked up on the swab and placed on a microscope slide. A special dye or stain is added, so that the doctor can see the cells better under a microscope. If cancer is present, some of these cells will be cancerous, and they look quite different from the normal cells.

In men, cancer occurs very frequently in the lungs and in the *prostate* (PROS-tate) gland, one of the male sex glands, situated near the bladder. Lung cancer kills more men than any other form of cancer. More than fifty thousand men die of lung cancer each year. But far fewer women die of this form of cancer. Why should this be so? Doctors believe that smoking is a major cause of lung cancer. And in general, men smoke more than women.

Each year more and more people get lung cancer. In fact, the number of cases of lung cancer is going up much faster than any other kind of cancer. Cigarette smoking seems to be the most important cause of lung cancer, although some scientists feel that it is not the only cause. They believe that air pollution may also help to cause cancer.

Another widespread type of cancer is skin cancer. Although many men and women get skin cancer, not too many die from this disease. It is much easier to detect and treat than cancers that occur deep within the body. Many people have warts or moles on their skin. In most cases these are benign tumors. But they may change into cancerous tumors. Indeed one of the warning signals of cancer is a sudden change in the size or color of a wart or mole.

Sometimes *pigment* (PIG-ment) cells in the skin become

cancerous. These pigmented or colored cancers are called *melanomas* (mell-a-NOE-muhz). They are the deadliest of all the skin cancers. They *metastasize* (meh-TAS-ta-size) very quickly, spreading to other parts of the body.

People who spend a great deal of time outdoors in the sun have a much higher chance of getting skin cancer. Sailors and farmers are two groups who get skin cancer more often than others. Sunlight contains invisible radiation called ultraviolet rays. These rays are very powerful. They are the part of sunlight that can produce a suntan or cause a painful sunburn. Ultraviolet rays can also cause *mutations* (mue-TAY-shunz) or changes in the DNA inside the cells. And some of these changes can turn a normal skin cell into a cancer cell.

Another place where cancer strikes very often in both men and women is the large intestine, the *colon* (COLE-un) and *rectum* (RECK-tum). More than 45,000 Americans die each year from these cancers. As in all other cancers, many of these people could have been saved if the cancer had been found sooner. For the earlier a cancer is discovered, the better the chance that it can be treated successfully.

Physicians and medical researchers are making steady progress against cancer. In the early 1900's, nearly everyone who got this disease died, in spite of doctors' attempts to save them. Now one out of every three cancer victims is saved. The American Cancer Society estimates that half of all the cancer victims *could* be saved, using the treatments we have now, if only their cancers were found or *diagnosed* (dye-ag-NOHSD) soon enough. And cancer researchers in their laboratories are constantly searching for new ways to treat and cure this disease.

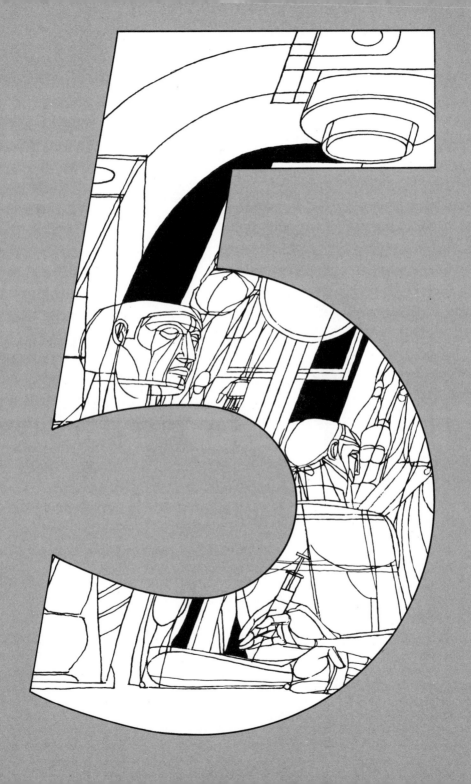

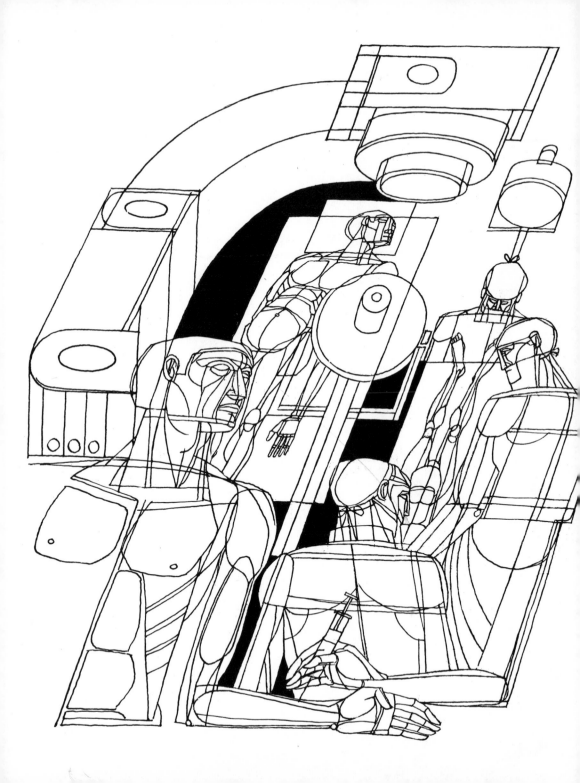

how cancer is treated

Medical researchers have found cures for many diseases. If you catch *pneumonia* (new-MOHN-ee-uh) you may be cured quickly with a shot of *penicillin* (pen-ih-SILL-in) or one of the other *antibiotics* (an-tee-bye-OT-ics). Other drugs can cure people who are infected with worms and other *parasites* (PAR-a-sites).

When doctors speak of cures for cancer they usually mean that the *symptoms* (SIMP-tums) have disappeared for at least five years. Nearly two million Americans alive today were successfully treated for cancer five or more years ago. Almost a million more have been treated successfully since then. And so, nearly three million people now living have been saved by treatments used by cancer specialists.

The three most important kinds of treatments are surgery, radiation, and *chemotherapy* (key-moh-THER-a-pee), treatment with chemicals.

The oldest type of treatment is surgery. Ancient records show that Egyptian doctors were using this method to treat cancer about 3,500 years ago. Surgery works best when cancers are discovered early. If a tumor is cut out before it has metastasized, the patient can be completely cured. In operating, the surgeon tries to make sure to get out all the cancer cells, even if this means taking out some of the normal tissues that the cancer has invaded. For if any cancer cells are left, they can begin to multiply again after the operation.

Even if a cancer has spread too far for a complete cure to be possible, surgery may still help the patient. If a tumor is blocking the intestines or the channels that carry the urine, an operation can open the passages, even if not all of the tumor can be removed. Surgery can also help to ease the great pain that cancer can bring.

Cryosurgery (cry-oh-SUR-jery)—supercold surgery—is a new technique that is being used more and more in the treatment of cancer. Instead of a knife, the surgeon uses a probe with a hollow channel containing liquid nitrogen. The nitrogen that makes up four-fifths of the air that we breathe is a gas. But if air is cooled down to -320 degrees Fahrenheit, the nitrogen turns into a liquid. Liquid nitrogen is so cold that tissues or other substances that come in contact with it rapidly freeze. In cryosurgery, a tumor can be cut out very rapidly, with practically no pain and bleeding at all.

Cryosurgery has some important advantages over ordinary surgery in the treatment of cancer. Less damage is done to the normal tissues, and the wounds heal better. In the ordinary kind of surgery, some cancer cells may break away and travel through the body. They may settle down in other organs and form new tumors. But in cryosurgery, this usually does not happen. The cancerous tumor is taken out very cleanly and does not get a chance to spread.

Modern surgeons are using another exciting new weapon against cancer that is almost the opposite of cryosurgery. They can destroy cancer cells with very sharply focused beams of hot light, made with a device called a *laser* (LAZE-er). The colored tumors of melanomas absorb more of the laser light than normal cells. Thus the laser beams kill only the colored cancer cells. Now doctors are trying to find dyes that will color the cells of other cancerous tumors, so that they too can be treated with laser beams.

Radiations of various types are very helpful, both in diagnosing cancers and in treating them. You may have had a chest X-ray. The X-ray machine was placed against your chest, and invisible radiations called X-rays passed through your body. They formed a picture on a photographic plate. By looking at the picture, a doctor can see the lungs and know whether any tumors are growing inside them. X-rays are also useful for detecting cancer in other parts of the body. Some-times a chemical that does not let X-rays pass is used to out-line an organ better in the X-ray picture and thus let the doctor see more clearly whether it is completely normal. A person may drink a mixture containing a *barium* (BARE-ee-um) compound for an X-ray examination of his stomach or intestines. Or a special dye may be injected into the body.

Radioactive *isotopes* (EYE-so-topes) can also be used in much the same way. The *thyroid* (THYE-royd) gland, for example, is an organ that helps to tell the body how fast to burn its food. This gland contains a great deal of iodine, and when we eat foods containing iodine, this chemical goes mainly to the thyroid gland. If a doctor suspects that his pa-tient may have a tumor of the thyroid, he can give the patient a mixture containing radioactive iodine to swallow. This is a form of iodine that continually sends out radiations. The radioactive iodine will go to the thyroid gland. Then the doctor can move a *Geiger counter* (GYE-ger COUNT-er), a device used to detect radiations, over various parts of the body to see just where the *radioisotope* (ray-dee-o-EYE-so tope) is. The amount of *radioactivity* (ray-dee-o-ak-TIV-ih-tee) in normal thyroid tissue is quite different from that in tumor tissue, and thus the doctor can tell whether there is a tumor in the gland and exactly where and how large it is.

The tiny amounts of radiations used in taking an X-ray picture or diagnosing a tumor with radioisotopes are safe. But larger doses of radiations can damage or even kill cells and tissues. They can make changes in the DNA of the cells, so that the information it contains is no longer quite right and the cell cannot do its jobs properly. Radiations can upset the body's ability to make new blood cells and can knock out its disease-fighting cells and organs. But since radiations can kill cells, they provide a powerful weapon against cancer cells. The big problem is to find ways to kill the tumor without killing the patient too.

Cancers of the skin and some other cancers that occur in a small, clearly outlined part of the body can be treated very well with beams of radiations from a machine located outside the body. An X-ray machine may be used. Or the doctor may use the radiations from radioactive *cobalt* (KOE-bault) or some other radioisotope. The beam of radiations can be focused very exactly to hit only the tumor tissue, just as you can focus the spray from a garden hose by turning the nozzle on the end.

A small portion of a radioisotope can also be inserted directly into the tumor. Or the patient may swallow or receive an injection of a radioisotope. Radioactive iodine, for example, can be used not only to diagnose, but also to treat cancer of the thyroid gland. For almost all of it goes to the thyroid gland, and the rest of the body thus does not receive its radiations. Radioactive *phosphorus* (FOSS-fer-us) is concentrated in the bone marrow, and it is used to treat certain kinds of leukemia.

Medical researchers are searching for drugs to use with

radiation treatments. They have found some chemicals that cause cells to be more easily damaged by radiations and other chemicals that help protect cells from radiations. Both types can be useful, in helping the radiations to kill off the tumors more effectively and in protecting the rest of the body from damage by radiations while the tumor is being killed. In fact, scientists hope that they will be able to find some chemicals that work both ways at the same time, making cancer cells more easily killed and protecting normal cells.

Some chemicals have been found to slow cancer growth or even to kill the cancer cells. One problem with most *anticancer* (an-tee-CAN-cer) chemicals is that they are poisonous to the normal cell as well as to the cancer cell. The reason that they can be used at all is that many chemical reactions usually take place at a much faster rate in cancer cells than in normal cells. And so the cancer cells take in more of the poisonous chemical than the surrounding normal cells do. But these anticancer drugs must be used carefully. For an *overdose* (OE-ver-dose) might make the patient ill or even kill him.

It was during World War II that modern research began in cancer chemotherapy, or treatment with chemicals. Scientists were experimenting with poison gases. They found that the mustard gas that had been used in World War I can interfere with the growth of cells. A very similar substance, called nitrogen mustard, turned out to be an effective drug that is still used to treat certain types of cancer, including some types of leukemia and lung cancer.

Studies of antibiotics have also yielded some drugs that can be used against cancer. The antibiotics *actinomycin D* (ak-tin-oh-MYE-sin DEE) and *daunomycin* (DAWN-oh-mye-sin) are not very effective in treating bacterial infections, for they cause too much damage to human cells while they are killing the bacteria. They can be used to treat leukemias and some other cancers.

Another form of chemotherapy that seems quite promising is the use of *antimetabolites* (an-tee-meh-TAB-oh-lytes). These are chemicals that are very similar to chemicals that the cell needs in order to live. If a cell takes in an antimetabolite, it is at first "fooled." The antimetabolite becomes bound to important chemicals of the cell. These chemicals cannot perform their normal tasks, and without them the cell cannot work properly. If there is enough of the antimetabolite present, the cell may die.

Some antimetabolites that are being used to treat cancer, especially leukemias, are *methotrexate* (meth-oh-TREX-ate), *6-mercaptopurine* (six mer-kap-toe-PURE-een), *5-fluorouracil* (five flure-oh-URE-a-sill), and *arabinosylcytosine* (a-rab-ih-noe-sil-SYE-toe-seen). These are all very similar to normal chemicals used by the cells. But the danger in using these compounds comes from the fact that they can also damage normal cells. Researchers are searching for chemical differences between normal cells and cancer cells. If they can find such differences, they will be able to make "magic bullets" that will kill cancer cells and leave normal cells alone.

45

Recently it seemed that researchers had found just such a "magic bullet." In studies of leukemia in mice, it was discovered that a substance from the blood *serum* (SEER-um) of guinea pigs stopped the growth of the cancer. In further studies it was found that certain leukemia cells and other cancer cells must have a supply of a chemical called *asparagine* (as-PAR-a-jeen) in order to live and grow. Normal cells can generally make all the asparagine they need. There is a substance, called *asparaginase* (as-PAR-a-jin-ace), which breaks down asparagine. This turned out to be the chemical in guinea pig blood that had stopped the mouse leukemia. It breaks down the asparagine in the blood of the leukemia victim before it can reach the cancer cells. Then the cancer cells are starved from a lack of this important chemical.

After many tests on animals, asparaginase was ready to be tried on humans. But it is a very complicated chemical, and there was no way at first to make large amounts of it in a very pure form. Researchers in Dallas, Texas, got together as much of the new drug as they could find and tried it on a nine-year-old boy who was dying of leukemia. The cancer disappeared, and the boy seemed to be cured. But then the supplies of the drug ran out. The leukemia flared up again, and the boy died.

The doctors believed that if they had only been able to give the boy larger doses of the drug, he could have been saved. Several chemical companies worked out new methods for producing large amounts of very pure asparaginase. But then came a disappointment. When the drug was tried on a large number of patients with leukemia and other cancers, it did not work as well as the researchers had hoped. For some of the normal body cells turned out to need asparagine after all, just as the cancer cells do, and large doses of the drug killed these important body cells too.

In addition, asparaginase is a protein, and it is usually obtained from bacteria, grown in enormous numbers in huge tanks. The human body has a very effective system for recognizing the differences between its own proteins and those of other organisms. If any "foreign" proteins enter the blood, the body's disease-fighting cells attack them. So when asparaginase is injected into a leukemia patient, a furious battle begins. The "foreign" protein is destroyed. And, just as many innocent civilians may be killed or injured in a war, the body's fight against asparaginase can result in harm to important organs, including the liver, kidneys, and the brain.

Some new methods give hope for getting around this difficulty. In one of these methods, developed by scientists at McGill University in Canada, tiny droplets of a liquid containing asparaginase are enclosed inside a very thin membrane like a plastic bag. This membrane is a little like a sieve, for it contains many tiny openings. The particles, or *molecules* (MOLL-eh-kyuls), of asparaginase are too large to pass through the openings. But asparagine is made up of much smaller molecules, and they can move freely in and out of the "microcapsules." Dr. T. M. S. Chang, at McGill University, placed microcapsules of asparaginase in a solution of asparagine. Soon all the asparagine was broken down, even though all the asparaginase was safely locked inside the microcapsules. Then he injected microcapsules with asparaginase into mice. He gave these mice, and a group of untreated mice, injections of tumor cells. The untreated mice all developed cancer. Many of the mice that received the microcapsules did not develop cancer at all. Indeed, this treatment was much more effective than just injecting a solution of asparaginase. For the asparaginase held inside the microcapsules could break down the asparagine of the blood without provoking an attack by the body's defense system.

The search for chemical cures for cancer goes on. In an enormous testing program, scientists have already tried out about a third of a million different compounds against cancer. First a chemical is tested on cancer cells growing in a test tube or *culture* (CULL-chur) dish. If it kills them or stops their growth, it is tried out on animals. Scientists can give mice and various other laboratory animals cancer by transplanting cancer cells from a tumor into their bodies. They have discovered some chemicals that cause cancers in a very high percentage of animals exposed to them. (One chemical, *benzpyrene* [benz-PYE-reen], produces cancerous tumors in *all* mice of a certain strain that are treated with it.) Some viruses have been found to cause cancer in animals. Researchers have also bred special strains of mice that almost always develop cancer of a particular type at a particular age. Only after a chemical has been found to be effective and safe in treating animal cancers is it tried on human cancer patients.

Anticancer chemicals have been found in plants from such far-off places as Brazil, China, and Madagascar. Skin-divers are searching the ocean bottoms and have found some promising drugs in clams and other sea creatures. Combinations of three and even four drugs used at the same time have been found to be more effective than any of the drugs used by themselves.

Charles B. Huggins won the Nobel Prize in Medicine in 1966 for learning how to use sex *hormones* (HOR-mones) in treating cancers. He found that female sex hormones helped to control cancers of the prostate gland in men. It was later found that male sex hormones can help in treating breast cancer in women.

The chemical war against cancer has barely begun. There is much to learn about the chemistry of the cancer cell. When these chemical mysteries are solved, cancer researchers may have cures for cancer.

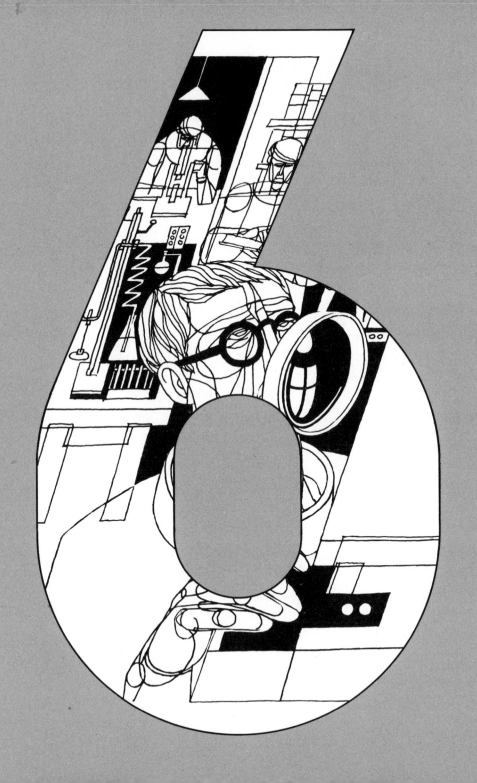

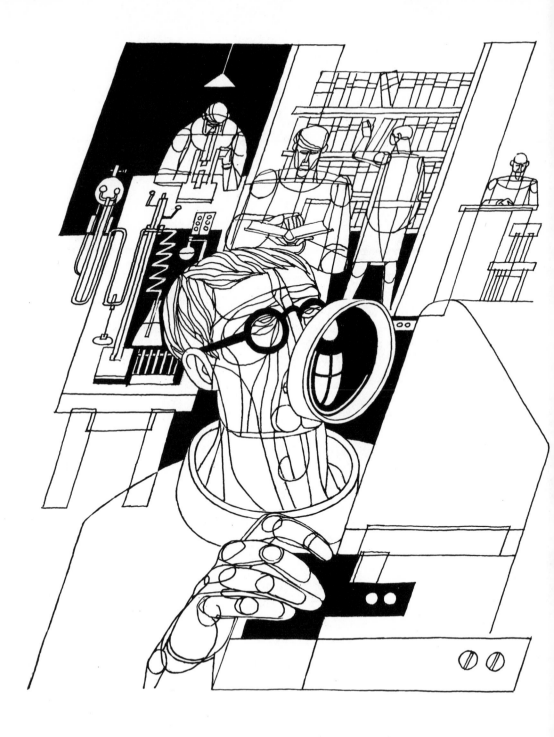

helping the body to help itself

Your body is in a constant war. A major defeat could mean death. Billions of invaders lie in wait on every part of your skin, the air you breathe, and the food you eat. At this very moment, in your blood, battles are raging. Countless numbers of white blood cells are attacking invading bacteria and gobbling them up. The smaller viruses are being dealt with by fast-acting proteins called *interferon* (in-ter-FEER-on), which keep them from multiplying too rapidly. Slower-acting proteins called antibodies also help in the fight.

These are the body's normal defenses against *infectious* (in-FECK-shus) diseases. The antibodies, although the slowest-acting, are the most important for providing long-lasting protection from disease germs. The body has a sort of "chemical sense," with which it recognizes all the tens of thousands of its own chemical substances. If a "foreign" chemical penetrates into the body, a series of reactions begins. Using the strange chemical as a pattern, certain cells of the body's defense system build up antibodies that fit it perfectly. Even after the chemical has disappeared from the body, some samples of the antibodies are kept on hand. Then if the body is invaded by this chemical again, the ready-made antibodies can be used as patterns for producing large supplies quickly.

The body can make antibodies against the chemicals that form the outer coats of bacteria and viruses. Once a supply of antibodies against a particular disease germ is on hand, the person is said to be *immune* (im-MUNE) to the disease that it causes. The body can also make antibodies against various other complicated chemicals that happen to get into the bloodstream. Sometimes this defense system works too well, and the person develops an *allergy* (AL-ler-gee) to some food or the pollen of a plant. His body is reacting to this harmless chemical as though it were a deadly germ.

Scientists believe that the body's *immunity* (im-MUNE-ih-tee) system can also work against cancer cells. For the cancer cells are different from normal cells, and if the body can recognize this difference, it can make antibodies against them. The researchers believe that this actually happens over and over again during a person's lifetime. Tiny cancers start to grow and then are recognized and killed off by the body's defenses. But if, somehow, the immunity system goes out of order, the body will fail to recognize that invading cancer cells are different and will not make any antibodies against them. If the defense system recovers before the cancer has spread too far, it can correct its mistake, and the cancer will stop growing or even disappear.

There is some good evidence that this actually does happen. Recently, surgeons have been perfecting methods of transplanting organs such as kidneys and even hearts into people whose own organs are badly damaged. Normally, the body would recognize that the transplanted organ contains many foreign chemicals and would make antibodies against them. Soon the transplant would shrivel up and die. This is called rejection. Transplant surgeons are therefore using drugs that temporarily knock out the body's immunity system. By the time it recovers and begins to make antibodies again, the transplanted organ has been a part of the body for so long that it may not seem so "foreign" anymore. Few or no antibodies against it are formed, and it is not rejected.

In using *antirejection* (an-tee-re-JECK-shun) drugs, doctors have to be very careful to protect their transplant patients from infections. For without their usual defenses against disease, even catching a cold could lead to death. Now they have discovered that transplant patients also have a much higher chance than normal of developing malignant tumors. This seems to show that the immunity system helps to protect normal people from cancer.

The idea that the immunity system is involved in cancer points the way to a whole new approach to the search for cancer cures. If the patient's immunity system can be strengthened and can be made to recognize that the cancer cells are foreign, then the body itself will fight against the cancer that threatens it.

Some doctors are testing drugs that stimulate the immunity system. Such substances have been obtained from the livers of sharks and even from the tissues of animals with cancer. In tests on animals, these chemicals seemed to work very well.

Other groups of researchers are trying to find ways to change cancer cells so that the body will know they are foreign. One group is adding poisons from bacteria to tumors. These poisons seem to "wake up" the body's defenses to fight the tumor cells as well.

Another group took tumor cells from dying human cancer patients and joined them chemically with a chemical, *gamma globulin* (GAM-ma GLOB-yew-lin), from the blood of rabbits. Then the doctors injected the substance back into the cancer patients. Their bodies formed three kinds of antibodies: antibodies against the rabbit gamma globulin, antibodies against the combination, and antibodies against their own tumor cells. Some of the patients were so close to death that they could not be helped. But in some the cancers seemed to be brought under control.

In still another immunity approach, a number of teams of medical researchers are trying to make vaccines against tumor cells. In one series of experiments on animals, baby rabbits, whose immunity system was not working yet, were injected with normal mouse cells. In this way they were fooled into recognizing the chemicals in normal mouse cells as their own and would not make any antibodies against them. Later, when their immunity systems were well developed, they were injected with mouse cancer cells. They made antibodies that would work against cancer cells but would not harm normal cells. When blood serum from these rabbits was injected into mice with cancer, the antibodies helped to fight the cancer.

Cancer vaccines may also come from people who have won their own fight against cancer. Sometimes, for no reason that doctors can find, cancer patients who are very ill—even dying—suddenly get better. Their tumors shrink and disappear, and no traces of cancer cells can be found in their bodies. These mysterious cures are called spontaneous remissions. Doctors are trying to find substances in the blood of such patients that will help to produce remissions in other cancer patients. They are also trying to find anticancer substances in the blood of healthy people, who have built up an immunity to various forms of cancer.

A Canadian scientist, Dr. Phil Gold, has been studying the blood of patients with cancer of the colon and rectum. In these blood samples he has found a special *antigen* (AN-tee-jen). (An antigen is a substance that stimulates the body to make antibodies.) This antigen seems to be made only by the cells of patients with cancer of the colon and rectum, and by the cells of unborn babies, growing inside their mother's body. It does not seem to be made by normal cells of healthy people. Dr. Gold hopes that a test for this special antigen will be a simple blood test that can be used to detect cancer of the colon and rectum. These types of cancer now kill about forty thousand Americans every year. But if they are caught early, before they spread, they can be removed, and the patients can be cured.

Many other researchers are also looking for chemical substances that can be used in tests for other kinds of cancer. One of the most exciting of these discoveries was recently announced by Dr. Chloe Tal of Israel. She found an antibody in the blood of cancer patients, which she named *tumor globulin* (TUE-mer GLOB-yew-lin) or "T-globulin." Dr. Tal tested the blood of 520 patients in various departments of her hospital. She found T-globulin in 356 of the blood samples. Then she checked the hospital records. Among the patients with positive tests, 350 had cancer that was found by other tests. Doctors suspected that three other patients had cancer, but they were not sure. The other three patients with positive T-globulin tests were pregnant women. Among the 164 patients whose blood did not contain T-globulin, not one had cancer. They had various other diseases, and one woman had a breast tumor that was not malignant.

Dr. Tal and other scientists are very hopeful that T-globulin can be used to develop a fast and simple test for many kinds of cancers. In Dr. Tal's tests, T-globulin was found in patients with 27 different kinds of cancers. Now Dr. Tal is trying to improve the test, so that a single drop of blood will be enough to tell whether a person has cancer. And such a test would be especially important, because it could be used to detect cancer in the very early stages, before it can be found by other methods. Twelve of the patients with a positive T-globulin test had not been diagnosed as cancer patients. When doctors first examined them, they did not seem to have cancer. But within a year, each of these patients was found to be suffering from cancer.

Someday T-globulin may also be used in a cure for cancer. Dr. Tal believes that the body makes this antibody when a cancer is first starting. T-globulin is a chemical that reacts with another, special chemical (an antigen) in cancer cells. Normal cells do not make this antigen. So the T-globulin goes straight to the cancer cells like a "magic bullet." If scientists can attach a poison to the T-globulin, they may be able to destroy cancer cells without harming normal cells.

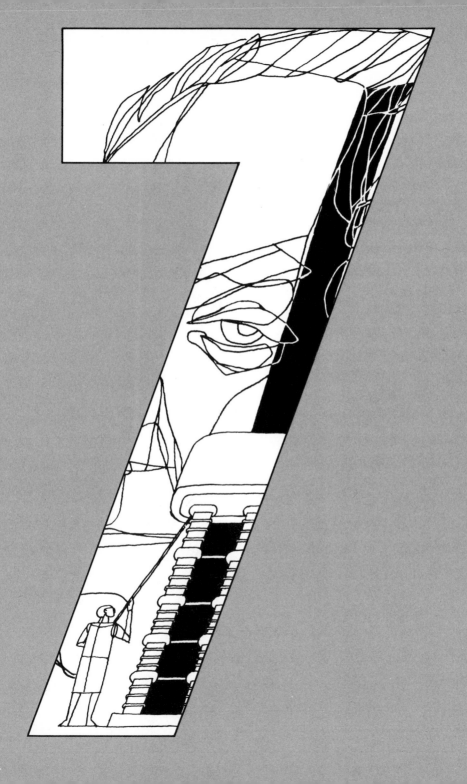

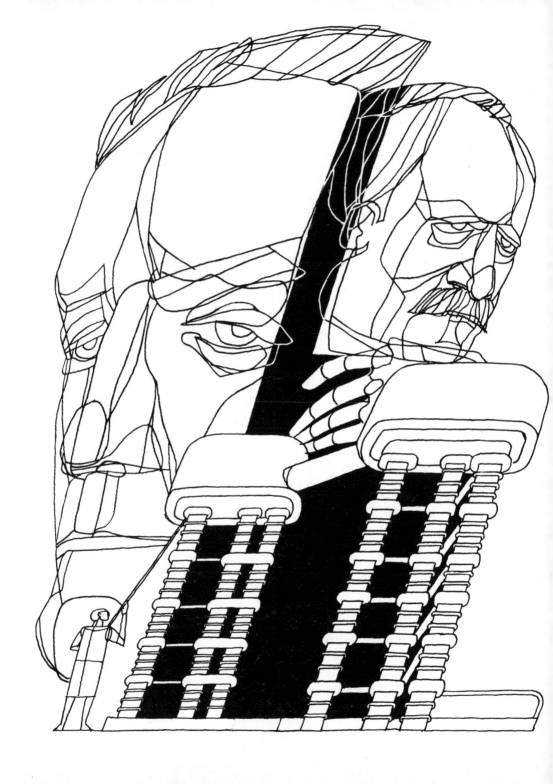

frontiers of cancer research

Our life depends upon the smooth cooperation of many different cells. A large number of complicated chemical reactions keeps each of these cells working normally. In cancer, some of these reactions go awry—they do not work as they should. If we could understand all the reactions that go on in a normal cell we would know just what cancer is and what causes it. We would probably soon have cures for it, too.

In thousands of laboratories throughout the world, scientists are studying the cell and the reactions that go on inside it. Each day new facts are learned. Each day the great puzzle of life becomes a little clearer. Of all of the methods that we

Human chromosomes

male   female

have mentioned or could mention, a study of the chemical reactions within cells and between cells is the most certain approach to the conquest of cancer.

One of the most promising pathways is to look for chemical differences between normal cells and cancer cells. If a chemical could be found in one and not the other, this difference might very well lead to control or cure for that cancer. The success of asparaginase in treating cancer is based on just such a difference. But the difference is not complete. Some normal cells, like cancer cells, cannot make asparagine and must get it from outside. Scientists know that some cancer cells cannot make *glutamine* (GLUE-ta-meen), an important chemical that normal cells can make. If it can be shown that all normal cells can make their own glutamine, then we may

64

have a cancer cure. For *glutaminase* (glue-TAM-in-ace), a chemical which breaks down glutamine outside of the cancer cells, would prevent them from getting any. And so the cancer cells would starve to death.

Scientists have found other chemical differences between some cancer cells and normal cells. Someday, when more is known about them, these may lead to controls or cures for cancers.

One researcher has discovered that tiny "bridges" called *cytopons* (SYE-toe-ponz) connect cancer cells. It is thought that some sort of chemical messages are sent across these bridges. When one cancer cell divides, all the cancer cells connected to it divide right afterward. The longer the bridge, the longer the next cell takes to divide. Normal cells do not form cytopons. If scientists can find some way to keep the cytopons from forming, they might be able to keep cancers from growing.

The surface of the cell holds important clues to the mystery of cancer. A normal cell stops growing when it comes in contact with the surface of another cell. Why do cancer cells keep on growing and dividing, piling up and crowding one another? There is something different about the surface of a cancer cell. Professor Max Burger at Princeton University has found a special protein in bean meal that sticks to the surface of certain kinds of cancer cells, like a chemical "band-aid." When the surface of a cancer cell is covered with this protein, which is called *concanavalin A* (con-ca-NAV-a-lin

AY), it stops growing wildly and turns back into a normal cell. If the "chemical band-aid" is taken off, the cell becomes cancerous again.

Dr. Burger believes that viruses may strip away part of the normal cells' covering, leaving "sticky spots" on the surface. These are the spots that are covered by concanavalin A. This chemical has not been tried out on living animals yet. It has only been tested in test tubes, on mouse cells that have been turned into cancer cells by treating them with a cancer-causing virus. Before scientists can know whether concanavalin A may really be a cancer cure, they must run many experiments to see whether it is effective in the living body. They must also find out whether it has any bad effects on normal cells, and on the systems of the body.

Researchers at the University of Minnesota are working on another difference in the surface of cancer cells that may someday bring a cancer cure. Cancer cells have more of a substance called *sialic* (sye-AL-ic) *acid* on their surface than normal cells do. Scientists have also found that a substance called VCN, taken from the bacterium that causes *cholera* (COLL-er-uh), can remove sialic acid from the surface of cells. The University of Minnesota research team removed some tumor cells from mice with cancer and treated these cells with VCN. Then they injected the cells back into the same mice. The tumors stopped growing, and in many of the mice they disappeared. The scientists believe that the large amounts of sialic acid on the surface of cancer cells prevent the body's immunity system from fighting these cells effectively. After VCN removes the extra sialic acid, the body makes antibodies against the cancer cells. When the doctors injected new tumor cells into the mice that recovered, the tumors did not grow. The mice were still protected.

Injections of cancer cells treated with VCN are a very specific treatment, that is, they work against only that one kind of cancer cells. They do not harm normal cells. The University of Minnesota doctors are now trying their new method on human cancer patients. They hope that they will be able to use the patients' own cancer cells to help fight their disease.

Just as the surface of the cell holds important secrets for solving the riddle of cancer, key clues are also to be found inside the cell, in the DNA.

The DNA of the cell is packaged in structures called *chromosomes* (CROE-moe-somes). Every normal human cell has 46 chromosomes. Cancer cells often have numbers that are different from this. One team of researchers believes that all cancer cells have too many of a certain kind of chromosome, called E16. This kind of chromosome seems to play a role in telling cells when to divide. And an important difference between cancer cells and normal cells is that they divide when they should not, forming great numbers of new cells.

More and more scientists are beginning to believe that viruses cause some and perhaps even most human cancers. It has been definitely shown that viruses cause cancer in many different kinds of animals. But this has not yet been definitely proven for human cancers, even though scientists have been trying for many years to find out if viruses cause human cancers.

Why are the scientists having so much trouble? There are many reasons. First of all, they cannot experiment with humans as they can with animals. No scientist would ever purposely do anything to a human that he thought might give him cancer. So he could never inject suspicious viruses into humans. And most viruses that attack humans do not grow well in other animals.

It has been found in studies with animals that viruses may stay dormant, or "asleep," inside cells for years before any signs of cancer appear. While the viruses are dormant, they are very difficult to find. For when a virus enters a cell, it leaves its protein coat behind. All that is left is DNA—DNA that looks very much like the DNA of the cell itself.

Scientists are working on a new technique for finding viruses inside cells. DNA is made of two long chains, which fit together like the two sides of a zipper. If the scientist suspects that a certain virus may be hiding in a cell, he "unzips" the DNA from a sample of the virus and then tries to match it to the DNA in the cell. If it matches exactly, it zips up onto the suspicious part of the cell DNA. Then the researcher knows that this part of the DNA in the cell came from the virus.

Indeed, scientists have performed just this kind of experiment with a type of cancer called Burkitt's *lymphoma* (lim-FOME-uh). This is a cancer of the lymph nodes, part of the body's disease-fighting system. (Perhaps you have noticed painful lumps in your neck when you had a bad cold. These were swollen lymph nodes, filled with special disease-fighting cells busily battling invading bacteria.) The DNA of a virus called the EB virus has been found "hiding" among the genes of Burkitt's lymphoma cells. The researchers believe that EB virus actually causes this kind of cancer.

Dozens of viruses have been found in other human cancer cells. But the fact that they are there does not mean that they do cause cancer. They just might happen to be there, without doing anything at all.

It is going to be very difficult for scientists to prove that viruses definitely do cause cancer in humans. If they do indeed play a role in cancer, they may very likely work together with radiations or with certain chemicals to change normal cells to cancer cells. And so the task becomes even more complicated. Nonetheless, the National Cancer Institute has just started a crash program in which scientists will try to prove, once and for all, whether viruses cause cancer in humans.

If scientists can prove that certain viruses do cause cancers, then they will probably be able to make vaccines to protect people from cancer just as we are now protected from smallpox, polio, and other virus diseases.

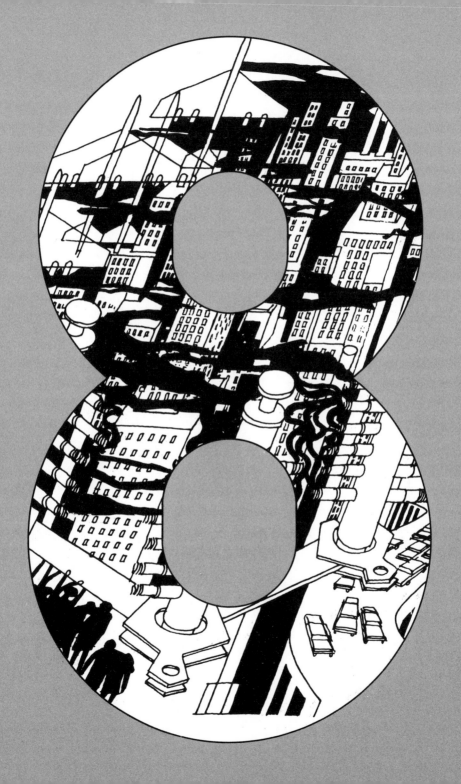

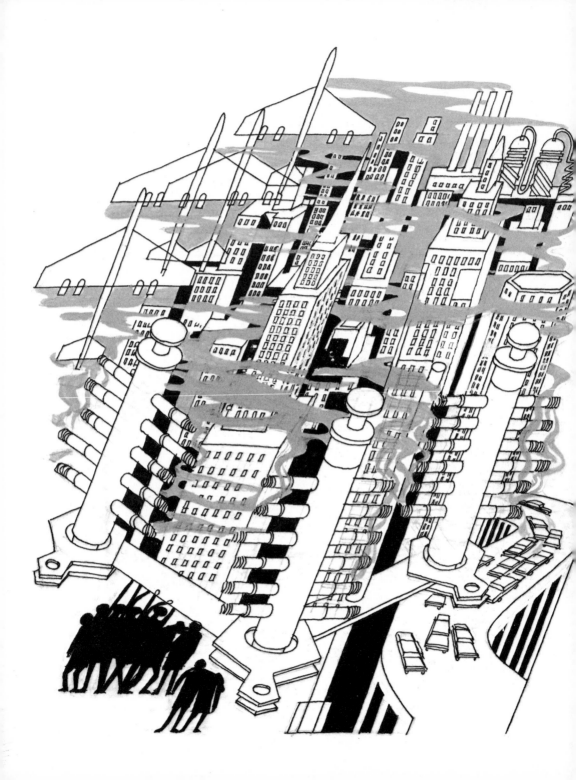

our dangerous world

Our world is polluted. Smoke and gases come from millions of cars and factories and homes all over our country. Tons and tons of poisons are poured out into the rivers and lakes, which become so polluted that nobody is allowed to swim in them. And the fish that are able to live in these waters become so poisonous that we are not allowed to eat them.

The *nitrogen oxides* (NYE-troe-jen OX-ides) from automobile exhausts and *sulfur oxides* (SUL-fer OX-ides) from the chimneys of factories and homes damage our lungs. The *carbon monoxide* (CAR-bun mo-NOX-ide) from both these sources gets into our blood. It is a poison that ties up oxygen so that the cells cannot use it. Without enough oxygen, the brain cannot work properly. So, in addition to causing damage to the body, carbon monoxide pollution probably causes many automobile accidents when the driver cannot think fast enough in an emergency. Other chemicals in the air, such as lead compounds, may damage the brain, the liver, and other important organs.

Since the first atomic bombs were exploded at the end of World War II, a new danger has been added to our world—radiation pollution. Our Earth has always had a certain amount of natural radiation, from rocks and soil and rays from the sun and from outer space. But atomic explosions produce large amounts of radioisotopes, which get into the water and soil and are taken up by plants and by animals that eat the plants. These radiations can cause cancer by changing the DNA and other substances in our cells. Most of the nations of the world have now agreed not to test nuclear weapons in places where they would add to the radiation pollution. But some radiations last a long time and are still around from the explosions and tests that took place before the treaty was signed. And now that atomic energy is being used for power plants and various other peaceful purposes, there is a danger that radiation pollution will increase.

Only now are people becoming concerned about the effects of all this pollution. And now the government at last is taking strong steps to cut down the poisons in the air, in drinking water, and in the foods that we eat.

It is not surprising that scientists have found many different carcinogens, or cancer-causing chemicals, in the polluted world we live in. For instance, every car that goes by gives off a little bit of benzpyrene. This chemical is such a strong carcinogen that scientists use it to cause cancer in animals when they want to try out new cancer treatments.

We even add chemicals that may be carcinogens to our food. Recently the Food and Drug Administration made food manufacturers stop using a compound called *cyclamate* (SYE-cla-mate) to sweeten foods when experiments on animals showed that it can cause cancer. Yet before the tests were conducted, millions of Americans drank "no-calorie" soft drinks sweetened with cyclamate and ate more of the chemical in cakes and candies and other foods. It was even used to cure bacon and added to children's vitamins.

Other possible carcinogens are still being added to our foods. *Sulfur dioxide* (SUL-fer dye-OX-ide) is used in food manufacturing, and *nitrites* (NYE-trites) are used in preserving coldcuts like corned beef and bologna. In the body, nitrites are changed into nitrous acid, which is a chemical that scientists use to produce mutations in cells in the laboratory. Mutations are changes in the DNA, and probably mutations are a cause of cancer.

Every time someone smokes near you, he is polluting the air you breathe with benzpyrene and other dangerous carcinogens. But although he is increasing the danger of your getting cancer, he is hurting himself far more. In 1962, the

Surgeon General of the United States Public Health Service set up a committee of scientists and doctors to study the relationship between smoking and health. After a long and careful study of all the scientific reports on smoking, the committee made its report. It stated that cigarette smoking is a cause of lung cancer, and pipe smoking can cause lip cancer. There also seems to be a relationship between smoking and cancers in other parts of the body. In addition to cancer, smoking can cause other diseases of the lungs and breathing passages and can be dangerous to people with heart trouble.

Since the Surgeon General's committee's report, a study sponsored by the United States government has brought more evidence that smokers have a much higher chance of dying from lung cancer than people who do not smoke.

Until recently, many smokers who did not want to quit could say, "Those studies are only statistics. Nobody has ever shown that smoking really causes cancer." That was true. For in humans, lung cancer takes so long to develop and people are exposed to so many other kinds of influences that scientists could not be completely sure that it was smoking that had caused a particular cancer. And they had not been able to try out smoking experiments on animals, because they could not get any animals to smoke cigarettes.

Finally, a group of scientists at the Veterans Administration Hospital in East Orange, New Jersey, trained some beagle dogs to smoke cigarettes. The smoke had to be pumped into the dogs' lungs at first. But then they grew to like smoking. Some of them became heavy smokers, smoking more than six thousand cigarettes in the test period of two and a half years. They even wagged their tails and begged for cigarettes.

At the end of the test period, the scientists examined the dogs. Many of the dogs that smoked got lung cancer or died from other lung diseases. In a group of dogs that did not smoke, none died at all, and none had lung cancer.

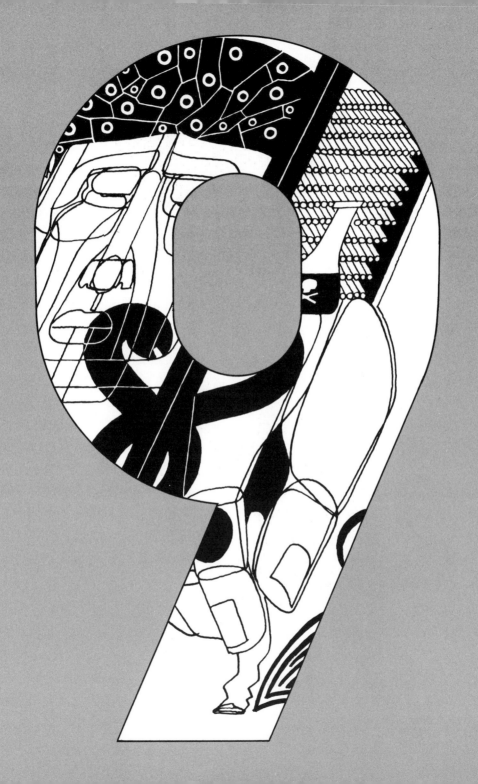

what you can do about cancer

Sometimes adults do not do the things they ought to. And sometimes they do things they ought not to.

For instance, does your father or mother or some other relative smoke? You know it is not good for them. And they know it too. What can you do?

Well, you can ask them to stop. Of course they probably will not listen to you. But then you can ask them to let you smoke. And of course they will not let you. Ask them why. They'll probably say it's no good for you. (If they say you are too young, ask them what age has to do with it, and then they will probably say it's no good for you.)

Now that they have admitted that smoking is not good for people, ask them if they will want you to smoke when you grow up. (They will probably say no.) Then ask them why they are setting such a bad example.

If you have gotten this far without a scolding, you might tell them that they can get more information about cancer, smoking, and how to stop smoking by writing to

The American Cancer Society
219 East 42nd Street
New York, N.Y. 10017

You might also tell them about the seven warning signals of cancer, drawn up by the American Cancer Society:

1. *Unusual bleeding or discharge.*
2. *A lump or thickening in the breast or elsewhere.*
3. *A sore that does not heal.*
4. *Change in bowel or bladder habits.*
5. *Hoarseness or cough.*
6. *Indigestion or difficulty in swallowing.*
7. *Change in size or color of a wart or mole.*

glossary-index

ACTINOMYCIN D (ak-tin-oh-MYE-sin DEE): An antibiotic that is used to treat leukemias and some other cancers. *45*

ALLERGY (AL-ler-gee): A reaction of the body's immunity system to some substance, such as a pollen grain, to which it has become sensitized. Antibodies are produced against the substance, and other systems of the body may be involved, resulting in a running nose or redness and swelling. *54*

ANEMIA (a-NEE-mee-uh): A condition in which the patient does not have enough red blood cells in his blood. Anemia may result from insufficient iron in the diet or a lack of certain vitamins. It may also result from serious diseases such as leukemia. *32, 33*

ANTIBIOTIC (an-tee-bye-OT-ic): A drug that kills disease microbes or keeps them under control long enough for the body's own defenses to fight them effectively. *39, 45*

ANTIBODY (AN-tee-body): A protein produced by the body's disease-fighting cells when a disease germ or some other "foreign" substance (called an antigen) invades the body. Antibodies combine with the germ or antigen and help the body's defenses to fight it more effectively. A special type of antibody is produced for each type of antigen. *53, 54, 55, 57, 58, 59, 67*

ANTICANCER (an-tee-CAN-ser) DRUGS: Drugs used to treat cancers. *44, 49, 57*

ANTIGEN (AN-tee-jen): A substance that stimulates the body to make antibodies. *58, 59*

ANTIMETABOLITE (an-tee-meh-TAB-oh-lyte): A chemical very similar to a substance, or metabolite, that the cell needs in order to live. If a cell takes in an antimetabolite instead of the metabolite it needs, it cannot function properly and may die. Drug researchers are searching for metabolites needed by cancer cells and disease germs but not needed by normal cells. Antimetabolites corresponding to such substances may be effective drugs. *45*

ANTIREJECTION (an-tee-re-JECK-shon) DRUGS: Drugs given to transplant patients to prevent rejection of the transplanted organ. These drugs also block the body's normal defenses against disease germs and leave the patient more susceptible to disease. *55*

APHID (AY-fid): A small insect with sucking mouthparts that lives on plant juices. *13*

ARABINOSYLCYTOSINE (a-rab-ih-noe-sil-SYE-toe-seen): An anti-metabolite used in the treatment of cancer. *45*

ASPARAGINASE (as-PAR-a-jin-ace): A chemical or enzyme that causes asparagine to be destroyed. *46, 47, 48, 64*

ASPARAGINE (as-PAR-a-jeen): An amino acid; one of the building blocks of the proteins. Many cells can make their own asparagine, but certain cancer cells cannot. *46, 47, 48, 64*

BACTERIUM (back-TEER-ee-um): A type of single-celled micro-organism. Many bacteria cause diseases, including tuberculosis, typhoid fever, and food poisoning. *14*

BARIUM (BARE-ee-um): A chemical element. Barium compounds are often used in X-ray examinations of the digestive system, because X-rays do not pass through them, and they produce a sharp outline of the digestive organs on the X-ray pictures. *42*

BENIGN (bee-NINE) TUMOR: A tumor that stops growing after it reaches a certain size and does not spread through the body. *27*

BENZPYRENE (benz-PYE-reen): A chemical that causes cancer in animals. Benzpyrene and other carcinogens are found in tars and burned fat. *48, 75*

CANCER (CAN-ser): A disease in which cells keep growing

when they would normally stop and divide more rapidly or more often than normal cells. A large mass of cells called a tumor may form, and the cancer cells may interfere with the work of normal cells. Cancer is one of the leading causes of death. *21*

CARBON MONOXIDE (CAR-bun mo-NOX-ide): A chemical compound containing carbon and oxygen. It can be carried by red blood cells and may prevent them from carrying oxygen to the body cells. *73, 74*

CARCINOGEN (car-SIN-oh-jen): A substance that causes cancer. *28, 75*

CARCINOMA (car-sin-OH-muh): A cancer that starts in covering tissues. Carcinomas occur in the skin and in the linings of the breathing passages and digestive system. *32*

CARTILAGE (CAR-ti-ledj): A tough gristlelike tissue. Cartilage gives shape to the nose and helps to support various bones of the body. The skeleton of a young baby is made up mostly of cartilage, which changes into bone as he grows older. *32*

CELL MEMBRANE (MEM-brain): The very thin membrane that surrounds each living cell. Food materials pass into the cell through the membrane, and waste products and other substances pass out through it. Certain important chemical reactions seem to take place at the cell membrane and the network of membranes within the cell that branches off from it. *20, 25*

CHEMOTHERAPY (key-moh-THER-a-pee): Treatment of a disease

with chemicals. *40, 44, 45*

CHOLERA (COLL-er-uh): A serious disease carried by bacteria found in contaminated drinking water. *66*

CHROMOSOMES (CROE-moe-somes): Structures within the nucleus of the cell containing the DNA, which carries the hereditary information of the cell. *67*

COBALT (KOE-bault): A chemical element. An isotope of cobalt, cobalt-60, is radioactive and is often used in medicine and industry as a source of radiations. *43*

COLON (COLE-un): The portion of the large intestine connected to the small intestine. *35, 57, 58*

CONCANAVALIN A (con-ca-NAV-a-lin AY): A protein that covers the surface of a cancer cell like a "chemical band-aid." Cancer cells in a culture, treated with concanavalin A, are transformed into normal cells. *65, 66*

CRYOSURGERY (cry-oh-SUR-jery): Supercold surgery: the use of extreme cold to cut through tissues with practically no pain and bleeding. *40, 41*

CULTURE (CULL-chur): A mass of cells or microorganisms grown in the laboratory in a test tube, a bottle, or a wide, shallow dish called a culture dish. *48*

CYCLAMATE (SYE-cla-mate): An artificial sweetener used in diet foods to replace sugar. Cyclamate was widely used in various foods consumed by the public until it was shown to cause cancer in experimental animals. *75*

CYTOPLASM (SYE-toe-plazm): The fluid that fills the cell (excluding the nucleus). *20*

CYTOPONS (SYE-toe-ponz): Tiny "bridges" that connect cancer cells and are believed to carry chemical messages between them. *65*

DEGENERATIVE (dee-JEN-er-eh-tiv) DISEASE: A disease caused by a gradual decrease in the efficiency of an organ or system of the body. The degenerative diseases that affect the heart and blood vessels are the greatest causes of death among Americans. *14*

DAUNOMYCIN (DAWN-oh-mye-sin): An antibiotic that is used to treat leukemias and some other cancers. *45*

DIAGNOSIS (dye-ag-NOHS-iss): The determination of the nature of a case of disease. *36*

DNA (DEE-EN-AY): Deoxyribonucleic acid. The chemical in which the hereditary information of the cell and of the whole organism is stored. It contains the "blueprints" for development and for nearly all the activities of the cell. *20, 21, 26, 27, 28, 35, 43, 67, 68, 74*

5-FLUOROURACIL (FIVE flure-oh-URE-a-sill): An antimetabolite used in the treatment of cancer. *45*

GAMMA GLOBULIN (GAM-ma GLOB-yew-lin): A group of chemicals in blood serum that contains disease-fighting substances. *56*

GEIGER (GUY-ger) COUNTER: A device used to detect and measure radiations. *42*

GENE (JEEN): The unit of heredity. Genes are made up of DNA, combined with proteins. They control the chemical reactions of the cell and determine the characteristics of the organism. *21*

GLUTAMINASE (glue-TAM-in-ace): A chemical or enzyme that causes glutamine to be destroyed. *65*

GLUTAMINE (GLUE-ta-meen): An amino acid; one of the building blocks of the proteins. Most normal cells can make their own glutamine, but certain cancer cells cannot. *64*

HORMONE (HOR-mone): A chemical substance that travels in the bloodstream and helps to control and regulate the chemical reactions of the body. *49*

INFECTIOUS (in-FECK-shus) DISEASE: A disease caused by germs such as viruses and bacteria and transmitted from one infected person to another. *53*

IMMUNITY (im-MUNE-ih-tee): A state of protection against a particular infectious disease. The body's disease-fighting cells have the "blueprints" for producing antibodies against the germ causing the disease, and they produce enormous numbers of these antibodies if this germ invades the body. *54, 55, 56, 57*

INTERFERON (in-ter-FEER-on): A protein produced by the body that acts rapidly to help fight invading viruses. *53*

ISOTOPE (EYE-so-tope): A variety of a chemical element. Isotopes of an element have the same chemical properties, but they differ slightly in weight and some other characteristics (for example, one isotope may be radioactive, while another isotope of the same element is stable and does not give off any radiations). *42*

LASER (LAZE-er): A device that provides an extremely sharply focused beam of very hot light. *41*

LEUKEMIA (lue-KEE-mee-uh): A cancer of the blood cells. In

leukemia, the body makes too many white blood cells, most of which never develop completely. Leukemia patients also have too few red blood cells in their blood. *32, 33, 43, 44, 45, 46, 47*

LYMPH (LIMF) NODE: A mass of tissue containing a large number of disease-fighting cells. Lymph nodes are found in the neck, the armpits, and various other parts of the body. They sometimes swell painfully during a cold or other disease. *69*

LYMPHOMA (lim-FOME-uh): A cancer of the lymph nodes. *69*

MALARIA (ma-LAIR-ee-uh): A disease that afflicts hundreds of millions of people throughout the world. It is caused by a tiny single-celled organism that is carried in the body of a mosquito and injected into human blood when the mosquito bites. *14*

MALIGNANT (ma-LIG-nent) TUMOR: A cancerous tumor that continues to grow and spreads through the body. *27, 56, 59*

MELANOMA (mell-a-NOE-muh): A pigmented cancer. Melanomas are the deadliest of all skin cancers. *35, 41*

METASTASIS (meh-TASS-ta-sis): The spread of cancer cells through the body, carried by the bloodstream. Some of these cancer cells may settle down in various parts of the body, forming new tumors. *27, 35, 40*

6-MERCAPTOPURINE (SIX mer-kap-toe-PURE-een): An antimetabolite used in the treatment of cancer. *45*

METHOTREXATE (meth-oh-TREX-ate): An antimetabolite used

in the treatment of cancer. *45*

MOLECULE (MOLL-eh-kyul): The smallest particle of a chemical substance that still has the chemical properties of that substance. *47*

MUTATION (mue-TAY-shun): A change in the DNA or hereditary material of the cell. A mutation in a cell that later develops into a new organism can produce a change in its characteristics, so that it is unlike its parents. Mutations can also cause cancer. *35, 75*

NITRITE (NYE-trite): A type of salt containing nitrogen and oxygen. Nitrites are used in preserving coldcuts but are changed in the body to a substance that may cause mutations and cancer. *75*

NITROGEN OXIDES (NYE-troe-jen OX-ides): Chemical compounds containing nitrogen and oxygen. They are an important part of pollution produced in automobile exhausts and other sources. *73*

NUCLEUS (NUE-klee-us): A structure within the cell that controls many of its activities. It contains DNA, the chemical in which the hereditary information of the cell and of the whole organism is stored. *20*

OVERDOSE (OE-ver-dose): Too large an amount of a drug or other substance used to treat a disease. The correct amount or dose of the substance can help the patient, but an overdose may have harmful effects. *44*

PAP SMEAR: A test for cancer of the uterus, in which cells obtained by wiping the entrance to the uterus with a cotton swab are treated with a special dye and studied under a microscope. The test is named after Dr. George Papanicolaou, who invented it. *33*

PARASITE (PAR-a-site): An organism that lives on or in the body of another type of organism, obtaining its nourishment from its "host." *39*

PENICILLIN (pen-ih-SILL-in): The first of the antibiotics, drugs that kill disease microbes. Penicillin is a substance produced by a type of mold. *39*

PHOSPHORUS (FOSS-fer-us): A chemical element; an important constituent of living matter. A radioisotope of phosphorous is used to treat certain kinds of leukemia. *43*

PIGMENT (PIG-ment): A colored substance. *34, 35*

PNEUMONIA (new-MOHN-ee-uh): A disease of the lungs, which often follows another illness such as influenza. *39*

PROSTATE (PROS-tate) GLAND: A male sex gland, situated near the bladder. *34, 49*

PROTEIN (PRO-teen): A type of chemical found in living things, made up of a long chain of amino acids. There are millions of different proteins in the living world. *28, 47, 53, 65, 68*

RADIATION (ray-dee-AY-shun): Rays of energy given off by atoms when they break down. *28, 41, 42, 43, 44, 69, 74*

RADIOACTIVITY (ray-dee-o-ak-TIV-ih-tee): The property of being radioactive, or giving off radiations. *42*

RADIOISOTOPE (ray-dee-o-EYE-so-tope): A variety of a chemical element that gives off invisible radiations, and is gradually transformed into a different isotope. *42, 43, 74*

RECTUM (RECK-tum): The portion of the large intestine follow-ing the small intestine. It is the last portion of the diges-tive tract through which undigested food materials and wastes pass before being eliminated from the body in the form of feces. The rectum is sometimes called the bowel. *35, 57, 58*

REJECTION OF TRANSPLANTS: An immunity reaction in which the body of a patient recognizes that the chemicals of a trans-planted organ are "foreign" and produces antibodies against it. The organ shrivels up and dies. *55*

REMISSION (ree-MISH-un): A temporary recovery from a dis-ease. During a remission, all the signs of the disease disappear, but they may return later. *57*

RNA (AR-EN-AY): Ribonucleic acid. A chemical form in which the hereditary information of the cell is carried. RNA is made by DNA, following the pattern of a portion of the DNA "blueprints." Several different types of RNA work together to build proteins. *28*

SARCOMA (sar-KOH-muh): A cancer that begins in connective tissue. Sarcomas occur in cartilage, muscle, and fatty tissue. *32*

SERUM (SEER-um): The liquid portion of blood obtained after the blood cells and other solid particles are removed. Blood serum may contain proteins that provide immunity to various diseases. *46, 57*

SIALIC (sye-AL-ic) ACID: A chemical compound. More sialic acid is found on the surface of cancer cells than on the surface of normal cells. *66, 67*

SULFUR DIOXIDE (SUL-fer dye-OX-ide): A chemical compound containing sulfur and oxygen. It is used in food manufacturing and is also a common air pollutant. It has been found to be a carcinogen. *75*

SULFUR OXIDES (SUL-fer OX-ides): Chemical compounds containing sulfur and oxygen. They are important pollutants formed in the burning of fuels. *73*

SYMPTOM (SIMP-tum): A sign of disease. A fever, running nose, and sore throat are symptoms of the common cold. A sore that does not heal or bleeding from the bowels may be symptoms of cancer. A study of the symptoms of the patient helps the doctor to diagnose his disease. *39*

THYROID (THYE-royd) GLAND: An organ found in the neck that helps to regulate the rate at which the body burns its food for energy. *42, 43*

TRANSPLANTATION OF ORGANS: An operation in which an organ, such as a kidney or heart, is removed from the body of one person and placed in the body of another person. It is connected there so that it can function normally in its new site. *55*

TUMOR (TUE-mer): A swelling or mass of tissue formed by cells that have grown more rapidly and divided more often than normal cells. *27, 32, 33, 40, 41, 42, 43, 44, 48, 56, 57, 59, 66*

TUMOR GLOBULIN (TUE-mer GLOB-yew-lin): An antibody in the blood of cancer patients which may be used in a test for various types of cancer. *58, 59*

ULTRAVIOLET (ul-truh-VYE-oh-let) RAYS: A form of radiation produced by the sun. Ultraviolet rays cannot be seen by human beings, although some animals, such as bees, can see them. The ultraviolet rays of the sun can cause a sunburn, can produce mutations in chromosomes, and can cause skin cancer. *28, 35*

UTERUS (YEW-ter-us): A pear-shaped organ in the abdomen, in which the baby develops before birth. *33*

VACCINE (vac-SEEN): A mixture containing disease germs that have been killed or changed in such a way that they no longer cause disease. A vaccine stimulates the body to produce antibodies against the disease. It is given to people to provide protection, or immunity, against the disease. *27, 57, 69*

VIRUS (VYE-russ): A type of microorganism, smaller than a bacterium. A virus is composed of an outer coat of protein and an inner portion of nucleic acid. Many viruses cause diseases, including measles, polio, influenza, and the common cold. *14, 27, 28, 48, 53, 66, 67, 68, 69*

about the authors

The husband-and-wife team of Alvin Silverstein and Virginia Silverstein has written more than twenty published books on science for young readers. Dr. Silverstein has been, since 1959, on the faculty of Staten Island Community College of the City University of New York, where he is now a professor of biology. He is chairman of the National Collegiate Association for the Conquest of Cancer. Mrs. Silverstein is a free-lance translator of Russian scientific literature and has worked as an analytical chemist. The Silversteins, who have six young children, live on a farm near Lebanon, New Jersey.

DATE DUE			
2			
9.			
11			
10			
12			

DATE	ISSUED TO
—	Laura Mowrer
2-23-19	Laura Mowrer
9-13-79	Mary Anne Gyle